Pearce

AF088190

by Iain Gray

Lang**Syne**
PUBLISHING
WRITING *to* REMEMBER

WRITING *to* REMEMBER

79 Main Street, Newtongrange,
Midlothian EH22 4NA
Tel: 0131 344 0414
E-mail: info@lang-syne.co.uk
www.langsyneshop.co.uk

Design by Dorothy Meikle
Printed by Printwell Ltd
© Lang Syne Publishers Ltd 2022

All rights reserved. No part of this publication may be reproduced, stored or introduced into a retrieval system, or transmitted in any form or by any means (electronic, mechanical, photocopying, recording or otherwise) without the prior written permission of Lang Syne Publishers Ltd.

ISBN 978-1-85217-666-2

Pearce

MOTTOS include:
I extend my right hand to the falling
(and) I am faced with the future
(and) Love nothing hard.

CRESTS include:
A demi-pelican
(and) A crane rising
(and) The mythical winged creature
known as a wyvern.

NAME variations include:
Pears
Pearse
Peerce
Peers
Peirse
Pierce

Chapter one:

Origins of Welsh surnames

by Iain Gray

***If you don't know where you came from, you won't know where you're going* is a frequently quoted observation and one that has a particular resonance today when there has been a marked upsurge in interest in genealogy, with increasing numbers of people curious to trace their family roots.**

Main sources for genealogical research include census returns and official records of births, marriages and deaths – and the key to unlocking the detail they contain is obviously a family surname, one that has been 'inherited' and passed from generation to generation.

No matter our station in life, we all have a surname – but it was not until about the middle of the fourteenth century that the practice of being identified by a particular, or 'fixed', surname became commonly established throughout the British Isles.

Previous to this, it was normal for a person to be identified through the use of only a forename.

Wales, however, known in the Welsh language as *Cymru*, is uniquely different – with the use of what are known as patronymic names continuing well into the fifteenth century and, in remote rural areas, up until the early nineteenth century.

Patronymic names are ones where a son takes his father's forename, or Christian name, as his surname.

Examples of patronymic names throughout the British Isles include 'Johnson', indicating 'son of John', while specifically in Scotland 'son of' was denoted by the prefix Mc or Mac – with 'MacDonald', for example, meaning 'son of Donald.'

Early Welsh law, known as *Cyfraith Hywel*, *The Law of Hywel*, introduced by Hywel the Good, who ruled from Prestatyn to Pembroke between 915 AD and 950 AD, stipulated that a person's name should indicate their ancestry – the name in effect being a type of 'family tree.'

This required the prefixes *ap* or *ab* – derived from *mab*, meaning 'son of' being placed before the person's baptismal name.

In the case of females, the suffixes *verch* or *ferch*, sometimes shortened to *vch* or *vz* would be attached to their Christian name to indicate 'daughter of.'

In some cases, rather than being known for

example as *Llewellyn ap Thomas* – *Llewellyn son of Thomas* – Llewellyn's name would incorporate an 'ancestral tree' going back much earlier than his father.

One source gives the example of *Llewellyn ap Thomas ap Dafydd ap Evan ap Owen ap John* – meaning *Llewellyn son of Thomas son of Dafydd son of Evan son of Owen son of John*.

This leads to great confusion, to say the least, when trying to trace a person's ancestry back to a particular family – with many people having the forenames, for example, of Llewellyn, Thomas, Owen or John.

The first Act of Union between Wales and England that took place in 1536 during the reign of Henry VIII required that all Welsh names be registered in an Anglicised form – with *Hywel*, for example, becoming Howell, or Powell, and *Gruffydd* becoming Griffiths.

An early historical example of this concerns William ap John Thomas, standard bearer to Henry VIII, who became William Jones.

In many cases – as in Davies and Williams – an s was simply added to the original patronymic name, while in other cases the prefix *ap* or *ab* was contracted to *p* or *b* to prefix the name – as in *ab Evan* to form Bevan and *ap Richard* to form Pritchard.

Other original Welsh surnames – such as Morgan, originally *Morcant* – derive from ancient Celtic sources, while others stem from a person's physical characteristics – as in *Gwyn* or *Wynne* a nickname for someone with fair hair, *Gough* or *Gooch* denoting someone with red hair or a ruddy complexion, *Gethin* indicating swarthy or ugly and *Lloyd* someone with brown or grey hair.

With many popular surnames found today in Wales being based on popular Christian names such as John, this means that what is known as the 'stock' or 'pool' of names is comparatively small compared to that of common surnames found in England, Scotland and Ireland.

This explains why, in a typical Welsh village or town with many bearers of a particular name not necessarily being related, they were differentiated by being known, for example, as 'Jones the butcher', 'Jones the teacher' and 'Jones the grocer.'

Another common practice, dating from about the nineteenth century, was to differentiate among families of the same name by prefixing it with the mother's surname or hyphenating the name.

The history of the origins and development of Welsh surnames is inextricably bound up with the nation's frequently turbulent history and its rich culture.

Speaking a Celtic language known as Brythonic, which would gradually evolve into Welsh, the natives were subjected to Roman invasion in 48 AD, and in the following centuries to invasion by the Anglo-Saxons, Vikings and Normans.

Under England's ruthless and ambitious Edward I, the nation was fortified with castles between 1276 and 1295 to keep the 'rebellious' natives in check – but this did not prevent a series of bloody uprisings against English rule that included, most notably, Owain Glyndŵr's rebellion in 1400.

Politically united with England through the first Act of Union in 1536, becoming part of the Kingdom of Great Britain in 1707 and part of the United Kingdom in 1801, it was in 1999 that *Cynulliad Cenedlaethol Cymru*, the National Assembly for Wales, was officially opened by the Queen.

Welsh language and literature has flourished throughout the nation's long history.

In what is known as the Heroic Age, early Welsh poets include the late sixth century Taliesin and Aneirin, author of *Y Gododdin*.

Discovered in a thirteenth century manuscript but thought to date from anywhere between the seventh and eleventh centuries, it refers to the kingdom of Gododdin that took in south-east Scotland and

Northumberland and was part of what was once the Welsh territory known as *Hen Ogledd*, *The Old North*.

Commemorating Gododdin warriors who were killed in battle against the Angles of Bernicia and Deira at Catraith in about 600 AD, the manuscript – known as *Llyfr Aneirin*, *Book of Aneirin* – is now in the precious care of Cardiff City Library.

Other important early works by Welsh poets include the fourteenth century *Red Book of Hergest*, now held in the Bodleian Library, Oxford, and the *White Book of Rhydderch*, kept in the National Library of Wales, Aberystwyth.

William Morgan's translation of the Bible into Welsh in 1588 is hailed as having played an important role in the advancement of the Welsh language, while in 1885 Dan Isaac Davies founded the first Welsh language society.

It was in 1856 that Evan James and his son James James composed the rousing Welsh national anthem *Hen Wlad Fynhadad – Land of My Fathers*, while in the twentieth century the poet Dylan Thomas gained international fame and acclaim with poems such as *Under Milk Wood*.

The nation's proud cultural heritage is also celebrated through *Eisteddfod Genedlaethol Cymru*, the National Eisteddfod of Wales, the annual festival of music, literature and performance that is held across the nation and which traces its roots back to 1176 when Rhys ap Gruffyd, who ruled the territory of Deheubarth from 1155 to 1197, hosted a magnificent festival of poetry and song at his court in Cardigan.

The 2011 census for Wales unfortunately shows that the number of people able to speak the language has declined from 20.8% of the population of just under 3.1 million in 2001 to 19% – but overall the nation's proud culture, reflected in its surnames, still flourishes.

Many Welsh families proudly boast the heraldic device known as a Coat of Arms, as featured on our front cover.

The central motif of the Coat of Arms would originally have been what was borne on the shield of a warrior to distinguish himself from others on the battlefield.

Not featured on the Coat of Arms, but highlighted on page three, is the family motto and related crest – with the latter frequently different from the central motif.

Echoes of a far distant past can still be found in our surnames and they can be borne with pride in commemoration of our forebears.

Chapter two:
Ancient bloodlines

A surname of Old French roots, 'Pearce' and its spelling variants that include 'Pierce', derives from the given name 'Pierre', a form of 'Peter' – which in turn derives from the Greek 'Petros', meaning 'rock.'

One reason for its popularity from the Middle Ages onwards is that this was the name bestowed by Jesus on his faithful disciple Simon – later St Peter – because of his resolute adherence to, and defence of, Christ's teachings.

Welsh forms of the surname are patronymic in origin, with 'ap Pirs', 'ap Pirs' and 'ap Pyro' indicating 'son of.'

Early bearers of the Pearce name were not identified with any particular one of the thirteen historic Welsh counties – although there was a strong association with North Wales, which boasts the seven counties of Anglesey, Caernarfonshire, Denbighshire, Flintshire, Merionethshire, Montgomeryshire and Radnorshire.

In common with many other Welsh people of today, flowing through their veins is a rich and heady brew of the blood of the ancient Britons and invaders in the form of Anglo-Saxons, Vikings and Normans.

Composed of the Jutes, from the area of the Jutland Peninsula in modern Denmark, the Saxons from Lower Saxony, in modern Germany and the Angles from the Angeln area of Germany, the Anglo-Saxons held sway in what became known as England and also in parts of Wales from approximately 550 to 1066.

They had usurped the power of the indigenous Britons – who referred to them as 'Saeson' or 'Saxones' – and it is from this that the Welsh term for 'English people' of 'Saeson', the Scottish- Gaelic 'Sasannach' and the Irish-Gaelic 'Sasanach' derive.

We learn from the *Anglo-Saxon Chronicle* how the religion of the early Anglo-Saxons was one that pre-dated the establishment of Christianity in the British Isles.

A form of Germanic paganism, with roots in Old Norse religion, it shared much in common with the Druidic 'nature-worshipping' religion of the indigenous Britons such as the Welsh.

It was in the closing years of the sixth century that Christianity began to take a hold in Britain, while by approximately 690 it had become the 'established' religion.

The first serious shock to Anglo-Saxon control came in 789 in the form of sinister black-sailed Viking ships that appeared over the horizon off the island monastery of Lindisfarne, in the northeast of England.

Lindisfarne was sacked in an orgy of violence and plunder, setting the scene for what would be many more terrifying raids on the coastline of not only England, but also of Wales, Ireland and Scotland.

Further invasion followed between approximately 950 AD and 1000 by the feared Northmen, and the coastline of Wales was repeatedly subjected to their raids – but, when not raping and pillaging, they established trading posts and settlements at modern day Haverfordwest, Fishguard and Caldey Island.

It was through intermarriage that the bloodlines of the native Britons such as the Welsh became infused with those of the Anglo-Saxons and the Vikings.

But there would be another infusion of the blood of the 'Northmen' in the wake of the Norman Conquest of 1066 – a key event in the history of the British Isles that sounded the death knell of Anglo-Saxon supremacy.

By 1066, England had become a nation with several powerful competitors to the throne.

In what were extremely complex family, political and military machinations, the monarch was Harold II, who had succeeded to the throne following the death of Edward the Confessor.

But his right to the kingship was contested by two powerful competitors – his brother-in-law King

Harold Hardrada of Norway, in alliance with Tostig, Harold II's brother, and Duke William II of Normandy.

In what has become known as The Year of Three Battles, Hardrada invaded England and gained victory over the English king on September 20 at the battle of Fulford, in Yorkshire.

Five days later, however, Harold II decisively defeated his brother-in-law and brother at the battle of Stamford Bridge.

But he had little time to celebrate his victory, having to immediately march south from Yorkshire to encounter a mighty invasion force led by Duke William that had landed at Hastings, in East Sussex.

Harold's battle-hardened but exhausted force confronted the Normans on October 14, drawing up a strong defensive position at the top of Senlac Hill and building a shield wall to repel William's cavalry and infantry.

The Normans suffered heavy losses, but through a combination of the deadly skill of their archers and the ferocious determination of their cavalry they eventually won the day.

Morale had collapsed on the battlefield as word spread through the Anglo-Saxon ranks that Harold, the last of their kings, had been killed.

William was declared King on December 25, and the complete subjugation of his Anglo-Saxon subjects followed – with those Normans who had fought on his behalf rewarded with their lands, a practice that was repeated in Wales.

Invading across the Welsh Marches, the borderland between England and Wales, the Normans gradually consolidated gains by building castles, for example in what they called 'Penfro' – later to lend its name to the town of Pembroke.

Under a succession of Welsh leaders who included Llywelyn ap Gruffudd, known as Llywelyn the Last, resistance proved strong.

But it was brutally crushed in 1283 under England's ruthless and ambitious Edward I, who ordered the building or repair of at least 17 castles and who in 1302 proclaimed his son and heir, the future Edward II, as Prince of Wales, a title known in Welsh as *Tywysog Cymru*.

Another heroic Welsh figure arose from 1400 to 1415 in the form of Owain Glyndŵr – the last native Welshman to be recognised by his supporters as *Tywysog Cymru*.

In what is known as The Welsh Revolt, he achieved an early series of stunning victories against Henry IV and his successor Henry V – until mysteriously disappearing from the historical record after mounting an ambush in Brecon.

Some sources assert that he was either killed in the ambush or died a short time afterwards from wounds he received – but there is a persistent tradition that he survived and lived thereafter in anonymity, protected by loyal followers.

During the revolt, he had consistently refused offers of a Royal Pardon and – despite offers of hefty rewards for his capture – he was never betrayed.

Chapter three:

Fame and infamy

Bearers of the Pearce name, in common with many others, have their fair share of skeletons in the closet – or, in the case of the convict, killer and cannibal Alexander Pearce, skeletons in the wild bush land of Tasmania.

The gruesome tale of the Irishman, who was born in Co. Monaghan in 1790, begins when the farm labourer was aged 29 and he was sentenced to penal transportation to Van Diemen's Land, now Tasmania, for stealing six pairs of shoes.

Working under forced labour in Hobart, he absconded and a £10 reward was offered for his recapture.

Caught shortly afterwards and charged with not only absconding but also forgery, a second order of penal transportation was imposed and he was sent to toil under the harsher penal regime at Sarah Island, Macquarie Harbour.

Along with seven other convicts – Edward Brown, Alexander Dalton, Thomas Bodenham, William Kennerly, Matthew Travers, Robert Greenhill and John Mather – Pearce escaped and he and his fellow escapees set out across the hostile West Coast of Tasmania.

After about fifteen days into their arduous trek across the unforgiving landscape and with their food supply having run out, the starving men in desperation drew lots to see which of them would be killed to provide food for the others.

Bodenham literally drew the short straw and he was summarily despatched by Greenhill with the axe he carried and which he jealously guarded.

After they had feasted on his body, Brown, Dalton and Kennerly, fearing a similar fate, left their companions and struck off on their own – with Kennerly and Brown thought to have returned later to the area of Macquarie Harbour and Dalton dying en route from exhaustion.

The axe-wielding Greenhill, along with Pearce, Mathers and Travers, continued on their gruelling journey and, again with no food, the next victim to fall was Mathers.

It appears that lots had not been drawn on this occasion.

Greenhill and Travers had been friends before their escape from Macquarie Harbour and had been sentenced to a second term of penal servitude after stealing a schooner in an attempt to escape from Hobart, and acted as a team.

With Mathers randomly selected by the pair for

the 'cannibal pot', Pearce was well aware that he could well be the next victim.

But Travers was bitten on the foot by a snake and, when it became clear that he would not survive, his erstwhile friend Greenhill killed him and he and Pearce cannibalised the body.

In what developed into a macabre game of cat-and-mouse, Greenhill and Pearce dared not even sleep.

But Pearce managed to prevail – grabbing Greenhill's axe in a moment when his guard was down, killing him and feasting on the body.

Reaching an area of settlement, Pearce joined a sheep-rustling ring, but the ring was rounded up and Pearce, after having spent a total of 113 days on the run from Macquarie Harbour, was returned there.

Within a year, however, he was on the run again – this time in the company of fellow convict Thomas Cox.

He was recaptured within ten days, but not before he had killed and cannibalised his hapless companion – with parts of Cox's body found in Pearce's pockets although he still had food left from when he had escaped.

He confessed to his grisly crimes and was hanged at Hobart Town Gaol in July of 1824 – chillingly stating just before his execution: "Man's flesh is delicious. It tasted better than fish or pork."

Meanwhile, he has been the subject of a number of books, folk songs, and drama-documentaries that include the 2008 *The Last Confession of Alexander Pearce* and the 2010 *Confessions of a Cannibal Convict*.

In contemporary times, another infamous bearer of the otherwise proud name of Pearce is Edgar Pearce – the 'Mardi Gra Bomber' who carried out a campaign of terror and extortion in the London area from December of 1994 until his arrest in April of 1998.

His targets were branches of Barclays Bank and the supermarket chain Sainsbury's.

Born in 1937 in Leyton, London, it was in a bid to extort money from the bank and supermarket that he placed crude home-made explosive devices in some of their branches.

Most of these failed to detonate, but those that did injured customers and staff with fortunately only one person seriously injured.

Often leaving a 'calling-card' featuring a photograph of two anonymous men wearing dark glasses and the message "Welcome to the Mardi Gra experience", he also spent six months stalking and photographing customers of Sainsbury's and threatening to target them with a high-powered crossbow if his demands for money were not met.

His plan was to withdraw the money through any one of the hundreds of cashpoint cards that he had demanded be issued in a computer magazine under the guise of a special promotion.

Unemployed at the time of his reign of terror and extortion – which had resulted in Barclays Bank having to spend an additional £140,000 on security and Sainsbury's £640,000 – Pearce had at one time worked in advertising, then as a restaurateur before he started a home renovations business, but the latter two enterprises failed.

Caught in an elaborate police 'sting' operation as he attempted to withdraw £700 from a cash-point at Whitton, London, it was stated at his subsequent trial at the Old Bailey – where he pled guilty – that he had hoped to carry out the perfect crime by utilising his advertising know-how.

His counsel, Nadine Radford QC, stated that her client had behaved irrationally because of a combination of factors that included heavy consumption of alcohol and suffering from a stroke that had left him with a form of brain injury.

She told the judge that he had not intended to injure anyone and that: "What he wanted was the completion of the grand plan. The object of the exercise was mental stimulation."

Convicted of actual bodily harm, unlawful wounding and possession of explosives and firearms and twenty charges of blackmail, the Mardi Gra Bomber was given jail terms totalling 224 years.

With these running concurrently, this means the actual sentence works out at 21 years.

A decidedly more respectable bearer of the Pearce name was Sir William Pearce, founder of the famed and former Fairfield Shipbuilding and Engineering Company on the Clyde.

Born in 1833 in Chatham, near Kent, he trained as a shipwright and a naval architect at Chatham Dockyard, where one of his first major responsibilities was supervising the construction of the mighty ironclad warship HMS *Achilles*.

Taking up the appointment in Scotland in 1863 of surveyor to the Lloyd's Register on Clydeside, by only a year later he was general manager of the shipbuilding and engineering firm R. Napier and Sons.

It was in this role, combining his technical skills with business acumen, that he designed transatlantic liners for the French Compagnie Générale Transatlantique, while in 1878 he became the sole owner of John Elder and Company – having become a partner nine years earlier.

Eight years after acquiring this company, the business was converted into the limited company the Fairfield Shipbuilding and Engineering Company, with Pearce as chairman.

Renowned for its development of the triple expansion engine and constructing vessels for shipping lines that included the Pacific Steam Navigation Company and the British and Africa Steam Company, the vast shipyard complex covered a bustling hive of noisy activity that covered more than 70 acres and employed up to 5,000 workers.

Not confining his activities solely to shipbuilding but also active in politics, Pearce was elected Conservative Party Member of Parliament (MP) for Govan in 1885.

He died in 1888, a year after being created Sir William Pearce, 1st Baronet, of Cardell, in the County of Renfrew.

Chapter four:

On the world stage

The only cast member of the Broadway production of *On the Town*, which ran from 1944 to 1946, to be included in the 1949 film of the name starring Gene Kelly, Alice Pearce was the American actress born in New York City in 1917.

It was after Kelly had seen her stage performance that he pressed for her to be included in the film.

She is best known, however, for her role from 1964 until her death in 1966 of the nosy neighbour Gladys Kravitz in the television comedy series *Bewitched*.

Born in 1967 in Ely, Cambridgeshire and settling with his family when he was aged three in Geelong, Victoria, **Guy Pearce** is the British-Australian actor who, in addition to television credits that include the soap *Neighbours*, has big screen credits that include the 1994 *The Adventures of Priscilla, Queen of the Desert*, the 2000 *Memento* and, from 2010, *The King's Speech*.

On British shores, **Eve Pearce** is the veteran Scottish actress born in Aberdeen in 1929.

Winner of a scholarship when she was aged

nineteen to study at the Royal Academy of Dramatic Art (RADA), her acting career began two years later with the Preston Repertory Theatre followed a year later with the Pitlochry Festival Theatre in her native Scotland.

Coming to wider public attention in the 1960s through her role as a squatter with a brood of children in the television soap *Coronation Street*, other television credits include *Please Sir!*, *Z-Cars*, *Taggart*, *Torchwood* and the mini-series *The 10th Kingdom*.

She has also performed in a number of Royal Shakespeare Company productions, while as a poet her *First Poetry Collection* was published in 2012.

Also on British shores, **Jacqueline Pearce** is the television and film actress born in 1943 in Woking, Surrey.

Her film credits include the 1965 *Sky West and Crooked*, the 1966 *Carry On* comedy *How to Get Ahead in Advertising* and the 1989 *White Mischief*, while her many television credits include the role from 1978 to 1981 of Servalan in the *Blake's 7* science fiction series, *The Avengers*, *Callan* and *The Young Indiana Jones Chronicles*.

Best known for his role of "Grandad" Trotter from 1981 until his death in 1984 in the sitcom *Only Fools and Horses*, **Lennard Pearce** was the actor of stage, television and film born in 1915 in Paddington, London.

Other television credits include *Dixon of Dock Green* and *Crown Court*, while his many stage credits include *Much Ado About Nothing* and *Rosencrantz and Guildenstern are Dead*.

An award-winning English entertainer, **Billy Pearce** was born in Leeds in 1951.

A former 'Redcoat' entertainer for the British holiday camp enterprise Butlins before embarking on the club circuit, he reached the final of the television talent show *New Faces* in 1986.

Host three years later of his own television series, *You Gotta Be Jokin'*, he was the recipient in 1994 of the British Comedy Award for Top Theatre Variety Performer, while he has also starred in a number of pantomimes.

Behind the camera lens, **Bobby Pearce** is the American stage, television and film designer born in 1961 in Miami.

Nominated for the Outer Critics Circle Award for Outstanding Costume Design and the Tony Award for Best Costume Design for the 2003 production of *Taboo*, starring Boy George, he has also acted as designer for films that include the 2009 *The Big Gay Musical*.

Born in 1975, **Drew Pearce** is the British film writer, director and producer whose film writing credits include the 2013 *Iron Man 3*, starring Robert Downey, Jr., while he was also the creator in 2007 of the cult television comedy *No Heroics*.

Born in London in 1980, **Lawrence Pearce** is the director and writer whose credits include the 2006 horror film *Night Junkies* and, from 2008, *Mixed Up*.

Bearers of the Pearce name have also excelled in the highly competitive world of sport.

In the boxing ring, **David "Bomber" Pearce** was the Welsh heavyweight champion born in 1959 in Newport, Monmouthshire; winner of both the Welsh and British heavyweight titles, he died in 2000.

Also in the boxing ring but in much earlier times, **Henry "Hen" Pearce** was the bare-knuckle prize fighter who – fighting under what were then the London Prize Ring Rules – was recognised as English champion from 1804 until his retirement in 1807.

Born in 1777 in Bristol, he was nicknamed "The Game Chicken" because of his habit of signing his name "Hen", rather than "Henry".

He died in 1809, while in 1987 he was posthumously inducted into the Ring Boxing Hall of Fame and, in 1993, the International Boxing Hall of Fame.

On the football pitch, **Chris Pearce** is the

Welsh former goalkeeper who, over a 14-year period, made 304 Football League appearances.

Born in 1961 in Newport, teams he played for include Blackburn Rovers, Rochdale, Port Vale and Burnley.

With the unusual distinction because of his parentage of having played for two different nations, **Alex Pearce** is the centre back born in 1988 in Wallingford, Oxfordshire.

Having made two international appearances for the Scotland Under-21 team and, at full international level, for the Republic of Ireland, he has spent his club career with Reading.

Winner of Player of the Season for Reading in the 2011-2012 Football League Championship, he has also played on loan for clubs that include Bournemouth and Norwich City.

In the wrestling ring, **Adam Pearce**, born in 1978, is the American retired professional wrestler who as a young man overcame Acute Muscular Compartment Syndrome in his lower legs to go on and win a succession of titles.

An inductee of the National Wrestling Alliance (NWA) Hall of Fame, his many titles include NWA World Heavyweight Champion on five occasions.

On the tennis court, **Brad Pearce** is the

American former tennis player who, after turning professional in 1986, went on to win four doubles titles during his career.

Born in 1966 in Provo, Utah, he is an inductee of the Intercollegiate Tennis Association (ITA) Hall of Fame.

On the golf course, **Eddie Pearce**, born in 1952 in Fort Myers, Florida, is the American golfer who won the 1968 U.S. Junior Open.

As a professional, he has played on the Professional Golf Association (PGA) Tour and The Players Championship, while in 1979 he finished second at the San Antonio Open.

On the athletics track, **Caroline Pearce** is the English athlete, sports presenter and sports model born in 1981.

Having competed for England in the World Pentathlon Championship when she was aged only 15, she also represented Great Britain in the 2005 World Bobsleigh Championship, while under the name of "Ice" she competed for a time in Sky One's relaunch of *Gladiators*.

From sport to the world of music, **Stephen Pearce**, nicknamed "Stevo", is the founder of the British record label Some Bizzare Records.

Born in 1962 in Haverhill, Suffolk, some of the

best-selling artists and bands he has signed include Depeche Mode and Soft Cell.

In the equally creative world of the written word, **Ann Philippa Pearce**, born in 1920 in Great Shelford, Cambridgeshire was the author of children's books best known for her 1958 fantasy novel *Tom's Midnight Garden*.

Winner of that year's Carnegie Medal from the Library Association, the 'time-slip' novel has since been adapted for the stage, television and film.

Author of other works that include her 1962 *A Dog So Small*, the 1978 *The Battle of Bubble and Squeak* and the recipient of an OBE, she died in 2006.

Specialising in global environmental issues, **Fred Pearce** is the English journalist and author born in London in 1951.

Environment consultant for *New Scientist* magazine and a contributor to a range of other publications that include *Time* magazine, *Popular Science*, the *Guardian* and the *Independent*, he is also the author of the 1989 *Turning Up the Heat: Our perilous future in the global greenhouse*.

One particularly colourful bearer of the Pearce name is Donald Mills Pearce, better known as **Donn Pearce**, the former soldier, merchant seaman and convict best known for his novel and screenplay *Cool Hand Luke*.

Born in Philadelphia in 1928, he left home when he was aged 15 and a year later attempted to join the United States Merchant Marine.

He was rejected because of his age but – again lying about his age – he opted for life as a soldier and was inducted into the U.S. Army, then embroiled in the Second World War, in 1944.

But, rebellious by nature, he became frustrated over what he thought were petty rules and accordingly went AWOL.

Turning himself in after only three days on the run, he was sentenced to 30 days in the stockade and then transferred to an infantry combat unit.

Now having second thoughts about life on the frontline, he wrote a letter to his mother who in turn contacted the army to inform them of her son's true age.

Thrown out of the army he was, however, by now old enough to join the Merchant Marine and this is what he duly did – later taking full advantage of what post-war Europe, particularly with regard to the black market, had to offer as his ship visited countries such as Spain, Portugal and France.

Turning his talents to counterfeiting American money, he was arrested and sent to prison in Marseilles after attempting to pass counterfeit bills. Ever resourceful, however, he managed to escape and make his way to Italy.

Forging new seaman's papers, he was signed on a ship bound for Canada – from where he crossed into the United States and pursued a new career as a safe-cracker and burglar.

Arrested for burglary in 1949, he endured two years of hard toil in the Florida Department of Corrections chain gangs – and it was this experience that inspired his best-selling 1965 novel *Cool Hand Luke*.

He also wrote the Academy Award- nominated screenplay for the film of the name, starring Paul Newman, while he even made a cameo appearance as the convict character "Sailor."

A contributor during the 1970s and 1980s to magazines that include *Esquire* and *Playboy*, the former convict turned best-selling author and screenwriter has also penned the 1972 novel *Pier Head Jump*, the 1974 *Dying in the Sun* and, from 2005, *Nobody Comes Back*.